SHARK SEARCH

In Search of Mako Sharks

Bonnie Phelps

PowerKiDS press

New York

Published in 2016 by The Rosen Publishing Group, Inc.
29 East 21st Street, New York, NY 10010

First Edition

Editor: Caitie McAneney
Book Design: Mickey Harmon

Photo Credits: Cover, p.1 (iron bars) Wayne Lynch/All Canada Photos/Getty Images; cover, pp. 1, 3, 4, 6, 8, 10, 12, 14, 16, 18, 20–24 (background) Ase/Shutterstock.com; cover (mako shark) Masa Ushioda/age fotostock/Getty Images; pp. 5, 9, 13 Ronald C. Modra/Sports Imagery/Contributor/Getty Images North America/Getty Images; p. 7 George Karbus Photography/Cultura/Getty Images; p. 11 (inset) Mogens Trolle/Shutterstock.com; p. 11 (main) Greg Amptman/Shutterstock.com; p. 14 Luis Carlos Torres/Shutterstock.com; pp. 15, 22 BryanToro/Thinkstock.com; p.17 Mark Conlin/Oxford Scientific/Getty Images; p. 19 Matt Jones/Shutterstock.com; p. 20 JULIE LUCHT/Shutterstock.com.

Library of Congress Cataloging-in-Publication Data

Phelps, Bonnie, author.
 In search of Mako sharks / Bonnie Phelps.
     pages cm. — (Shark search)
 Includes index.
 ISBN 978-1-5081-4343-7 (pbk.)
 ISBN 978-1-5081-4344-4 (6 pack)
 ISBN 978-1-5081-4345-1 (library binding)
 1. Mako sharks—Juvenile literature. 2. Sharks—Juvenile literature. I. Title.
 QL638.95.L3P54 2016
 597.3'3—dc23
                                        2015027133

Manufactured in the United States of America

CPSIA Compliance Information: Batch #BW16PK: For Further Information contact Rosen Publishing, New York, New York at 1-800-237-9932

Contents

The Mighty Mako

What's that darting through the water? It's the mako shark—the fastest shark **species** in the world. The mako shark's body is thin and pointed, like a **torpedo**. It can swim over 20 miles (32 km) per hour for long periods of time. Some makos dart through the water at much faster speeds.

Mako sharks are also known to put up a fight. They're armed with several rows of long, sharp teeth. Luckily, they'd rather hunt fish than people.

A mako shark's teeth point back inside its mouth. That helps it grab and hold slippery fish.

Shortfin and Longfin

There are two kinds of makos—longfin makos and shortfin makos. They both have sharp teeth that show even when they close their mouth. They both have **gills** to breathe and fins to swim. Both are silver-blue on the top of their body with a lighter belly.

What's the difference between the mako species? Longfin makos have larger eyes and **pectoral fins** than shortfin makos. Longfin makos are also darker around and under their **snout**.

Shortfin makos have white skin under and around their snout, while longfin makos have darker skin there.

gills

snout

pectoral fin

shortfin mako

Superspeed

The mako shark has special skin. It may look smooth, but it's actually covered in tiny points that help it slice through water. Along with its torpedo-shaped body, this helps the mako swim very quickly. The mako also has a very strong tail to **propel** it through water.

Makos use their speed to hunt unlucky **prey**. Few fish can outrun the mako. One mako shark was recorded swimming at around 50 miles (80.5 km) per hour!

The mako swims so fast that it can jump up to 20 feet (6 m) out of the water!

Keeping Warm

Mako sharks, like all sharks, are fish. But unlike most other fish, mako sharks are warm-blooded. Cold-blooded fish take on the temperature of their surroundings. In cold water, they're cold, and in warm water, they're warm.

However, mako sharks are warmer than the water they swim in. They can trap heat inside their bodies. Because makos can keep their muscles warm, they can swim quickly after their prey. Their muscles are ready for action when they see a fish swim by!

Another warm-blooded shark is the great white. These shark cousins are both fearsome hunters!

mako shark

great white shark

Finding a Mako

Where can you find a mako shark? They live in ocean waters all around the world. However, they prefer warmer water and stay out of very cold waters. Many live in the western Atlantic Ocean.

Makos mostly hunt in deep waters away from the shore. They can be found nearly 500 feet (152 m) underwater, where much of the food they eat swims. However, they're also known to hunt near the water's surface.

When they're chasing prey, makos sometimes get close to shore. That's bad news for swimmers!

On the Hunt

Luckily for swimmers, mako sharks would rather eat fish any day. They're **carnivores**. They hunt swordfish, tuna, squid, and other sharks. Many of their prey are very fast swimmers, so it's a good thing the mako is fast!

Swordfish may be tasty, but it's a **dangerous** dinner to catch. It has a long, sharp snout it uses like a sword. Makos can be hurt in a fight with this fish. Sometimes hunting a swordfish is a fight to the death!

swordfish

 The mako can travel nearly 40 miles (64 km) a day chasing after its prey.

Predator Pups

Makos can grow up to 13 feet (4 m) long. They can live to be around 30 years old. Yet these huge sharks start out as tiny babies.

The mother mako carries eggs inside her body. The babies come out of the eggs after 15 to 18 months. Then, the mother gives birth to around 8 to 10 live babies, which are called pups. Each one is around 2 feet (0.6 m) long. Once they're born, the mother doesn't take care of them. They have to learn to live and hunt on their own.

Mako pups sometimes eat each other while they're still inside their mother's body!

Mako Dangers

Like many other sharks, the mako is at the top of the **food chain.** This means it hunts many prey, but has no natural predators. A fish has to be big and fast to make a mako its dinner!

People are the greatest hunters of the mako. Some people like to eat it. Some like to hunt it for sport. Since the mako puts up a fast and fearless fight, people think it's fun to hunt.

People also hunt the mako shark for its fins, which are used in a Chinese soup.

Makos and People

The mako is a very **aggressive** hunter and known to put
a fight. But is it a danger to people?

It's very rare for a mako shark to attack a human. The
ko doesn't hunt people, and most bites are a mistake.
wever, if makos are **provoked**, they'll
end themselves. They've been known
urt fishermen. If a mako shark gets
ght in a fishing line, it will
t and bite its way out.

Sharks have more to fear from
people than people have to fear
from sharks.

SHARKS
NO
SWIMMING

Shark Bites!

 Mako sharks have been known to travel up to nearly 1,300 miles (2,092 km) in just one month.

 Mako sharks can swim in short bursts up to nearly 50 miles (80 km) per hour.

 Mako sharks need to swim all the time in order to stay floating in water. That's because they don't have a body part called a swim bladder, which many other fish have.

 Mako shark pups already have teeth when they're still in their mother's body.

 The largest makos can weigh up to 1,257 pounds (570 kg).

 Mako sharks tear their prey into pieces before swallowing.

Makos in Trouble

It may seem like this fearsome fish has nothing to worry about. However, mako populations are falling fast. People are catching and killing too many. Also, a mother mako has few babies in her life. That means it takes a long time for the number of makos to grow.

Luckily, rules have been put in place about how many makos can be caught each year. Spreading knowledge about this super shark helps keep it safe, too. Hopefully, the mako shark will speed through the oceans for many years to come.

Glossary

aggressive: Showing a readiness to attack.

carnivore: An animal that eats only meat.

dangerous: Unsafe.

defend: To keep something safe.

food chain: A line of living things, each of which uses the one before it for food.

gill: The body part that ocean animals such as fish use to breathe in water.

pectoral fin: Either of the fins of a fish that are on its sides.

prey: An animal hunted by other animals for food.

propel: To push or drive something onward.

provoke: To cause to become angry.

snout: An animal's nose and mouth.

species: A group of plants or animals that are all the same kind.

torpedo: A rocket-shaped exploding device that travels through water.

Index

Websites

Due to the changing nature of Internet links, PowerKids Press has developed an online list of websites related to the subject of this book. This site is updated regularly. Please use this link to access the list: www.powerkidslinks.com/search/mako